PROJECTS

Dorling Kindersley Readers is a compelling new reading programme for children, designed in conjunction with leading literacy experts, including Cliff Moon M.Ed., Honorary Fellow of the University of Reading. Cliff Moon has spent many years as a teacher and teacher educator specializing in reading and has written more than 140 books for children and teachers. He reviews regularly for teachers' journals.

Beautiful illustrations and superb full-colour photographs combine with engaging, easy-to-read stories to offer a fresh approach to each subject. Each *Dorling Kindersley Reader* is guaranteed to capture a child's interest while developing his or her reading skills, general knowledge, and love of reading.

The four levels of *Dorling Kindersley Readers* are aimed at different reading abilities, enabling you to choose the books that are exactly right for each child:

Level 1 – Beginning to read
Level 2 – Beginning to read alone
Level 3 – Reading alone
Level 4 – Proficient readers

The "normal" age at which a child begins to read can be anywhere from three to eight years old, so these levels are intended only as a general guideline.

No matter which level you select, you can be sure that you are helping children learn to read, then read to learn!

www.dk.com

Project Editor Carey Combe
Art Editor Mandy Earey
Senior Editor Linda Esposito
Senior Art Editor
Diane Thistlethwaite
Production Melanie Dowland
Jacket Designer Dean Price
Picture Researcher Liz Moore
Illustrator Peter Dennis

Reading Consultant
Cliff Moon M.Ed.

Published in Great Britain by
Dorling Kindersley Limited
9 Henrietta Street
London WC2E 8PS

2 4 6 8 10 9 7 5 3 1

A CIP catalogue record for this book is available
from the British Library

ISBN 0-7513-2852-9

Colour reproduction by Colourscan, Singapore
Printed and bound in China by L.Rex Printing Co., Ltd.

The publisher would like to thank the following for their kind
permission to reproduce their photographs:

a=above, c=centre, b=below, l=left, r=right, t=top

AKG London: 4–5; **Bilderdienst Suddeutscher Verlag gmbH**:
42tl, 44t, 47cr; **Corbis UK Ltd**: 2b, 43, 44–5, 46–7; **Hulton Getty**:
15tr, 15br, 19tr, 25, 32–3; **Popperfoto**: 1, 33tr, 37tr. 38–9; **Tony
Stone Images**: Alan R Moller 20b; **Topham Picturepoint**: 5tr, 17,
29br; **Ullstein Bilderdienst**: 9, 26b.

Contents

DK DORLING KINDERSLEY *READERS*

READING
3
ALONE

ZEPPELIN

THE AGE OF THE AIRSHIP

Written by Andrew Donkin

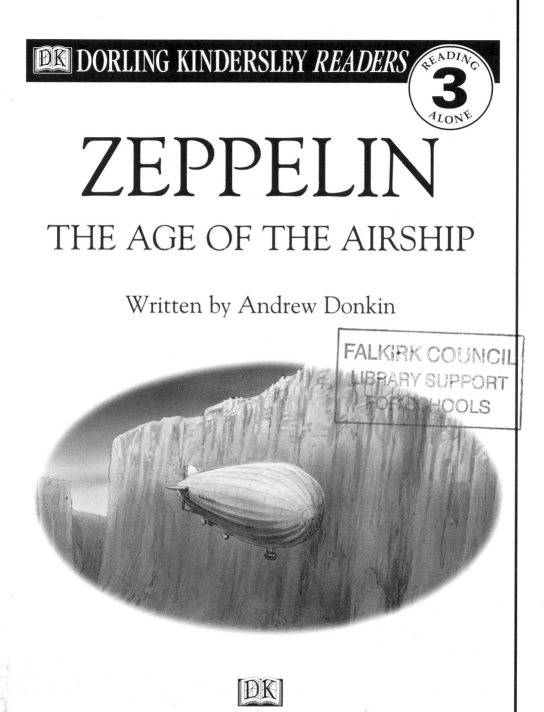

DK

London • New York • Sydney • Delhi
Paris • Munich • Johannesburg

The crazy count

"There he is! That's the count!"

The large crowd at the edge of Lake Constance in Germany parted slightly to allow a small figure to pass through.

Count Ferdinand von Zeppelin looked just like a mad inventor with his shock of white hair and long, droopy mustache. He had spent the last two years building his own airship. Today he would fly the airship for the first time. It was July 1900 and the idea of a man in the air seemed close to a miracle.

Could his invention really work?
"We fly at six o'clock!" he shouted.
A small boat slowly pulled the airship out of a floating hangar. The crowd gasped as the airship came into view – she was more than 140 metres long!

The airship was known as *Luftschiff Zeppelin One* or *LZ-1* for short. Her huge cylindrical shell was filled with hydrogen – a very deadly gas.

"It looks like a gigantic silver caterpillar," said a voice from the crowd.

The count rowed out to the huge machine and stepped carefully into one of the little cars that hung under the craft's long body.

At last, *LZ-1* was ready to launch!
"Drop the tow ropes!" ordered the count.
Everyone held their breath as the
anchor ropes fell away. Slowly, the *LZ-1*
rose from the water and into the air.
The crowd went wild with excitement.

The flight lasted 20 minutes, reached
heights of more than 3,700 metres, and
took the count a distance of 6 kms. The
LZ-1 was a success. She could fly!

The count was thrilled with his ship's performance and gave a huge party to celebrate the successful flight.

The *LZ-1* flew twice more. Then the count built two new ships – *LZ-2* and *LZ-3* – both designed for better flying. His dream of a future where airships filled the sky was starting to come alive.

Even the German government was interested and set the count a test. If he could build an airship that could fly non-stop for 24 hours, they would give him the money to build more.

So the *LZ-4* was born.

Zeppelin fever

Following the successful test flights of *LZ-3*, German shops started selling Zeppelin clothes, biscuits and sweets in the shape of tiny airships.

On August 4, 1908, the *LZ-4* took off from Lake Constance on her crucial 24-hour mission. It was a huge news event and all Germany awaited the outcome.

The flight got off to a bad start when an overheated engine delayed takeoff. However, against all expectations, the ship passed the gruelling 24-hour test.

But suddenly disaster struck. In front of the huge crowd, a violent gust of wind ripped the ship from its mast.

The *LZ-4* was smashed against nearby trees and she exploded in a ball of fire.

Count Zeppelin was devastated. Was this the end of his long-cherished dream? The German people didn't think so. Money started pouring in – everyone loved his airships and wanted him to build more. In fact, the count received so much money that he could begin work on another craft immediately.

The age of the airship had arrived.

How airships work

Early airships used a simple gas bag filled with hydrogen to lift them off the ground. Hydrogen is a gas that is lighter than normal air – so anything filled with hydrogen floats.

Mooring cone

Rigid skeleton

An airship's speed and height were controlled from the control car.

Passengers were able to look out of a viewing window.

Count Zeppelin had the brilliant idea of putting several gas bags inside one huge sausage-shaped skeleton made of metal. So if one or more gas cells sprang a leak, the craft could still fly.

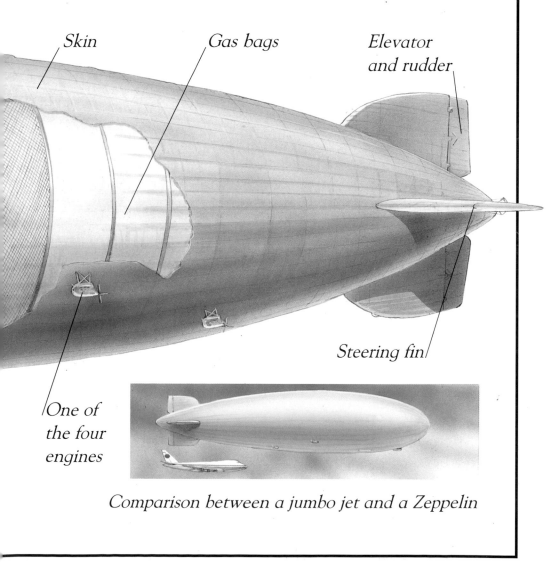

Skin

Gas bags

Elevator and rudder

Steering fin

One of the four engines

Comparison between a jumbo jet and a Zeppelin

Across America

It was September 3, 1923. A huge and excited crowd waited patiently on the windswept tarmac at Lakehurst Air Station in New Jersey. America's first airship, the *Shenandoah*, was about to depart on her maiden flight!

Amid cheers from the crowd, the *Shenandoah* lifted off. The hour-long flight was a complete success and America became gripped by *Shenandoah* fever. Everybody wanted to see America's first airship with their own eyes.

To satisfy public demand, a fantastic voyage was planned. The *Shenandoah* would fly from coast to coast, covering an incredible 14,000 kms – the first time this trip had ever been attempted.

Could it be done?

The Shenandoah *was initially called ZR-1*

Cow bags

The gas bags found in most airships were made from cows' stomachs. The skin was scraped clean and then glued onto linen panels.

At dawn on October 7, four hundred sailors gently pulled the *Shenandoah* from her hangar. At a word from her captain, they released the tow ropes and watched the mighty ship power away into the clear sky above them.

"Standard speed," ordered Commander Lansdowne as the craft headed west towards Washington, D.C. Right on schedule, and to the delight of those on the ground, the *Shenandoah* glided gracefully over the White House.

On the third day, the tall dark shape of the Rocky Mountains came looming into view. The *Shenandoah* would have to fly through many narrow mountain passes. The slightest mistake in steering would bring disaster. Crossing these would be the *Shenandoah*'s ultimate test.

The Shenandoah *in its hangar for maintenance*

It was getting dark as the airship reached the dangerous mountain passes. Every crew member was on duty, and each of the ship's five engines had a pair of engineers watching them. People darted in all directions, checking the gas bags and inspecting the structure. The smallest error during the next few hours could spell disaster for the whole ship.

Tied high

Tall landing masts were used to moor airships. From here the airship could be pulled down to the ground by ropes tied to the ship.

With nerves on edge, they approached the first pass. Suddenly they heard a thud. Trees had ripped away the radio antenna underneath – they were too low!

"Take her up another 100 metres," ordered the commander. Grateful for their narrow escape, he carefully steered the 200-metre-long ship along one twisting mountain canyon after another.

At last, they sighted the lights of San Diego and the Pacific Ocean beyond. The mountains were behind them – they were safe! The *Shenandoah* had become the first airship to fly from coast to coast.

Stormy weather

The age of airships was a period of great triumphs almost always followed by terrible disasters.

The year after the *Shenandoah*'s successful cross-country flight, the airship was sent on a goodwill mission to the Midwestern United States. The area is known for its violent storms, and Commander Lansdowne told his bosses that the weather might be too bad to fly safely, but they ignored his advice.

On a calm September day in 1924, the *Shenandoah* began her fateful journey.

Tornado alley
The Midwest is famous for its extremely violent storms and destructive tornados. The storms often cause massive damage to property.

Later that day, a storm was seen in the distance. Lansdowne quickly changed course. But suddenly, without warning, a gust of wind pushed the ship upward. Lansdowne struggled to control her but the storm tossed her around like a toy.

Suddenly the wind dropped and the *Shenandoah* began to plunge back towards the earth. She was falling at a stomach-churning 500 metres a minute. Wires started to snap under the strain and the skin of the ship began to tear.

Then she was caught by another upward current and lifted high in the sky once more. Could the ship survive such punishment?

The crew clung on in terror as the giant ship was twisted by the wind. Then, with a terrible ripping sound, the airship's hull broke into pieces.

A few seconds later, the control car was torn from its position beneath the front section of the ship. Lansdowne and seven of his crew plummeted straight to their deaths below.

23

Amazingly, and against the odds, the two largest sections of the airship stayed in the air. Then the tail section, with 22 men on board, plunged towards earth. But as it fell it straightened out and, luckily, also slowed down. The final crash into trees left the men stunned, but alive.

But the smaller forward section did not fall to earth. It began to rise again. The seven men trapped on board could do nothing as air currents carried them up to 3,048 metres. They were so high that the ground was nothing but a blur.

However, the men had been well trained. They began releasing helium from the gas bags and emptying the tanks of fuel. Somehow, they made the ship spiral gently downwards in ever-increasing circles and land safely in a field.

This tragedy did not only claim lives, it also destroyed the airship's reputation. People began to question the safety of these amazing flying machines.

The tangled remains of the Shenandoah

The top of the world

Roald Amundsen had become world-famous for being the first man to reach the South Pole. But he was always looking for new challenges, and now he fixed his sights on conquering the North Pole.

The intrepid Norwegian had already tried to fly over the North Pole. But he crash-landed, and spent 25 days on the freezing ice before he was rescued.

For his second attempt, Amundsen decided to use an airship, and he struck a deal with an Italian pilot named Umberto Nobile.

A dog's life

The crew of the *Norge* was made up of 16 men and one dog. Nobile insisted that his little terrier, Titina, come with him!

Together they would fly Nobile's airship, the *Norge*, from one side of the world to the other, flying directly over the North Pole and travelling over what was then unmapped territory.

Early on the morning of May 11, 1926, Amundsen, Nobile and their crew of 14 set off into the unknown.

The *Norge* made good progress at first, moving north at a steady 80 kilometres an hour. Then a bank of thick, freezing fog descended and the ship's instruments began to freeze up. Quickly, Nobile increased the height of the *Norge* until she sailed above the fog into sunshine.

As the craft neared the North Pole, the skies cleared over the ice and excitement built among the crew.

"Stand by to drop the flags," ordered Amundsen. They dropped their national flags as a symbolic gesture of reaching the Pole. The flags were weighted at one end so that they would stick in the ice. The Norwegian flag went first, followed by the Italian and lastly the American. All three sank firmly into the ice and fluttered in the wind.

But their journey wasn't over. The most dangerous part still lay ahead.

Mussolini's mission
The Italian dictator Mussolini was so excited about this trip over the North Pole that he personally gave Nobile a full-sized Italian flag to drop.

No-one knew what lay between the North Pole and Alaska. The group was travelling over ground no human being had ever seen before.

Suddenly, freezing fog engulfed them once more and the airship was soon covered in a dangerous coating of ice.

Every few minutes a piece of ice broke off and fell onto the ship's spinning propellers. The propellers turned each piece into a hail of deadly ice bullets and fired them at the ship's outer shell.

The crew rushed desperately around the airship, frantically repairing the holes in the outer fabric.

Finally, after two days without sleep, they sighted Alaska. But just when they thought they were safe, they spotted a huge ice storm approaching the ship from behind. Engines roared as the *Norge* raced to beat it. They landed just as the storm broke around them, but it didn't matter – they were safe. It was the most daring flight ever by an airship.

Hanging on a string

The American airship *Los Angeles* was the *Shenandoah*'s sister ship. This craft gave many passengers the most memorable ride of their lives – although not all of them wanted it!

At midnight on March 2, 1928, the ground crew at Lakehurst, New Jersey, waited for the arrival of the *Los Angeles*. It had been a long day and once the huge airship was safely in her hangar they could all go home.

Commander Rosendahl brought the ship slowly into position until she hovered just off the ground. A snowstorm was brewing as the ground crew grabbed the landing ropes. Those under the control car took hold of the hand rail.

Then, suddenly, things went wrong.

A powerful gust of wind hit the ship and, without warning, she started to rise.

"Let go of the lines!" shouted Commander Rosendahl as he felt the airship being swept upward.

The ground crew quickly dropped the ropes they were holding and in a matter of seconds the *Los Angeles* had disappeared into the snowstorm above.

Commander Rosendahl gave the order to restart the ship's huge engines.

As soon as he was in control of the ship, he relaxed and looked out of the window at the snowstorm surrounding them.

"Good heavens!" he cried.

Clinging desperately to the hand rail attached to the outside of the control car were eight members of the ground crew. The ship was now more than 200 metres in the air!

"Quick, get those men inside!" yelled the horrified commander.

Donald Lipke, a junior seaman, was the first to react. He punched his fist through a window and climbed out onto the rail. Freezing wind and snow blasted into Lipke's face. Quickly, he pushed the man nearest to him inside. Then, edging along the rail, he grabbed another man, and then another.

Bottoms up
A strong breeze while the *Los Angeles* was moored led to this freak accident where the ship's tail lifted 90 degrees into the air.

Soon, only one terrified man remained outside. Lipke crept slowly towards him. The man's fingers were numb with cold.

Suddenly the man lost his grip and slipped. Thinking quickly, Lipke dived towards him. Lipke just managed to grab his coat, preventing the young man from falling to his death below. Dragging the man in, Lipke collapsed on the floor.

The commander checked with the landing field and learned that all the missing men had been pulled on board – everyone heaved a huge sigh of relief.

The death of a dream

On the afternoon of May 6, 1937, New York City came to an unexpected halt. Traffic stopped and people rushed to their windows to gaze upward.

Floating silently and gracefully over the city was the sleek silver form of the *Hindenburg*. She was making her first trip of the new season, flying from Germany to America.

Having already completed one year of transatlantic flights, the future looked rosy – 18 more flights were scheduled – and the ship had a superb safety record.

Leaving New York, the ship set course for Lakehurst Station in New Jersey. As Lakehurst came into view, the passengers onboard prepared for touchdown.

Everything seemed absolutely perfect. What could possibly go wrong?

Inside, the *Hindenburg*'s passengers were comfortable and very relaxed. The huge ship was as well known for its sumptuous and luxurious accommodation as it was for its impressive safety record.

Its many spacious rooms included the promenade, where huge windows gave passengers fantastic views, the quieter reading room, and the dining room where musicians played live music.

This beautiful ship always drew a crowd of onlookers, often hoping to see inside. Some were friends and family of passengers, others were reporters coming to see the ship make another landing. From the promenade decks, people waved to the spectators below.

With a faint rumble from her four engines, the silver airship glided towards the mooring mast.

It was exactly 7.25 in the evening, and excitement grew as the waiting crowd watched the craft complete a sweeping turn on its final approach.

The engines were put into reverse and the giant airship came to a graceful halt.

Landing ropes were dropped and the 141 people that made up the landing crew took a firm hold.

It looked as though the *Hindenburg* was safely home again.

But suddenly, to the crowd's horror, flames erupted from the rear of the ship.

The wall of bright orange flame spread with great speed.

"It's burst into flames!" gasped one horrified radio reporter.

As fire leapt along the body of the ship, the landing crew directly under the burning Zeppelin ran for their lives.

Passengers trapped on board the doomed craft began to jump – many while the ship was still hundreds of metres in the air.

Suddenly the ship exploded and began to break up, crashing to the ground. Men, women and children ran screaming from the deadly inferno.

People were pulled from the twisted ruins of the ship. Some were barely injured. Others were terribly burned.

Thirty-six people lost their lives in the fire. The terrible photographs and film footage of the disaster shocked people all over the world.

In just 34 seconds the *Hindenburg's* impressive safety record vanished in smoke – and with it went the public's confidence in the safety of airships. The age of the airship was finally over. Count Zeppelin's dream was dead.

Looking for clues

Theories to explain the disaster include a bomb, a gas leak and, the most likely, the extreme flammability of the fabric cover on the ship.

Glossary

Air current
A strong flow of air in one direction.

Cabins
Small rooms where crew and passengers can rest and sleep during the flight.

Elevator
Device that controls an airship's height above the ground during flight.

Fuel tanks
Large containers in which the fuel for the engines is stored.

Gas
A substance which is neither solid nor liquid, such as oxygen and helium.

Gas bags
Inflatable sacks containing gas.

Ground crew
Airfield staff on the ground to help with an airship's landing. The crew might number hundreds of men and women.

Hangar
A huge building where aircraft are stored.

Helium
A gas that is lighter than air.

Hindenberg
The largest airship ever built. She exploded on May 6, 1937, in New Jersey.

Hull
The surface area of an airship's body.

Hydrogen
A lighter-than-air gas that explodes when exposed to flame.

Landing ropes
Long, strong ropes dropped down from the airship as it prepares to land. They are grabbed by the ground crew and used to pull the craft gently to earth.

Los Angeles
American airship also known as the "Pride of the Navy".

LZ1
The name that was given to the first airship that Count Zeppelin built in 1900. *LZ-1* actually stood for *Luftschiff Zeppelin One*.

Mooring mast
The place where an airship lands.

Mooring cone
Device on the nose of an airship that connects it to a mooring mast.

The Norge
An airship that flew over the North Pole.

Promenade deck
The area on board an airship where passengers can walk around.

Rudder
A flat blade at the rear of an airship that controls its direction.

Shenandoah
American airship that completed a trip across the USA.

Tornado
A violent, destructive wind storm.

Zeppelin
An airship that flies by using gas bags held in place by solid supports. It was named after Count Ferdinand von Zeppelin.